# WHAT MAKES MUSICIANS SO SARCASTIC?

# Peanuts® Parade Paperbacks

1. Who's the Funny-Looking Kid with the Big Nose?
2. It's a Long Way to Tipperary
3. There's a Vulture Outside
4. What's Wrong with Being Crabby?
5. What Makes You Think You're Happy?
6. Fly, You Stupid Kite, Fly!
7. The Mad Punter Strikes Again
8. A Kiss on the Nose Turns Anger Aside
9. Thank Goodness for People
10. What Makes Musicians So Sarcastic?
11. Speak Softly, and Carry a Beagle
12. Don't Hassle Me with Your Sighs, Chuck

# WHAT MAKES MUSICIANS SO SARCASTIC?

Cartoons from *Peanuts Every Sunday* and *It's a Dog's Life, Charlie Brown*

## by Charles M. Schulz

Holt, Rinehart and Winston / New York

Published simultaneously in Canada by Holt, Rinehart
and Winston of Canada, Limited.

First published in this form in 1976.

Library of Congress Catalog Card Number: 76-8677

ISBN: 0-03-018111-9

Printed in the United States of America

10 9 8 7 6 5 4 3 2

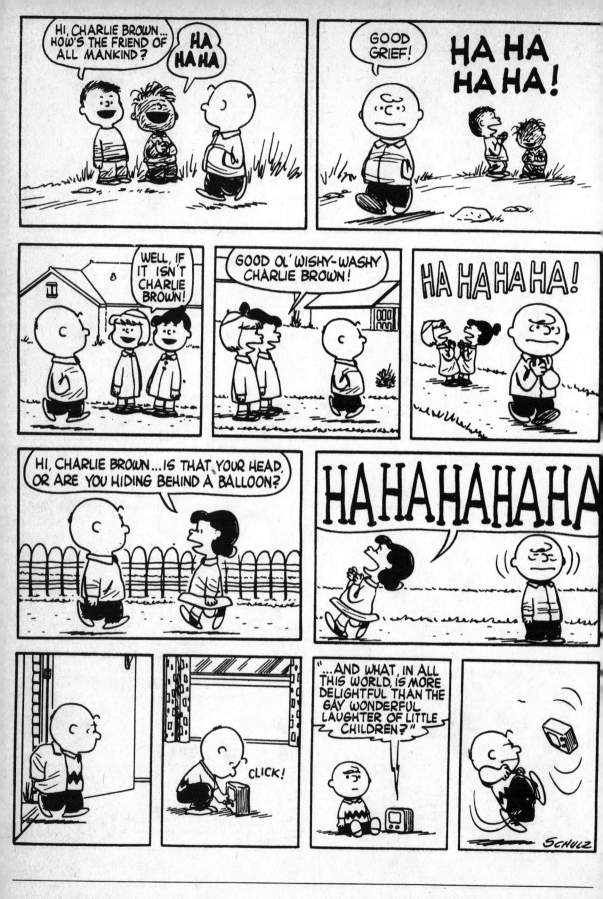

IT ALWAYS COMES AS A SHOCK WHEN IT HAPPENS TO SOMEONE YOU KNOW...

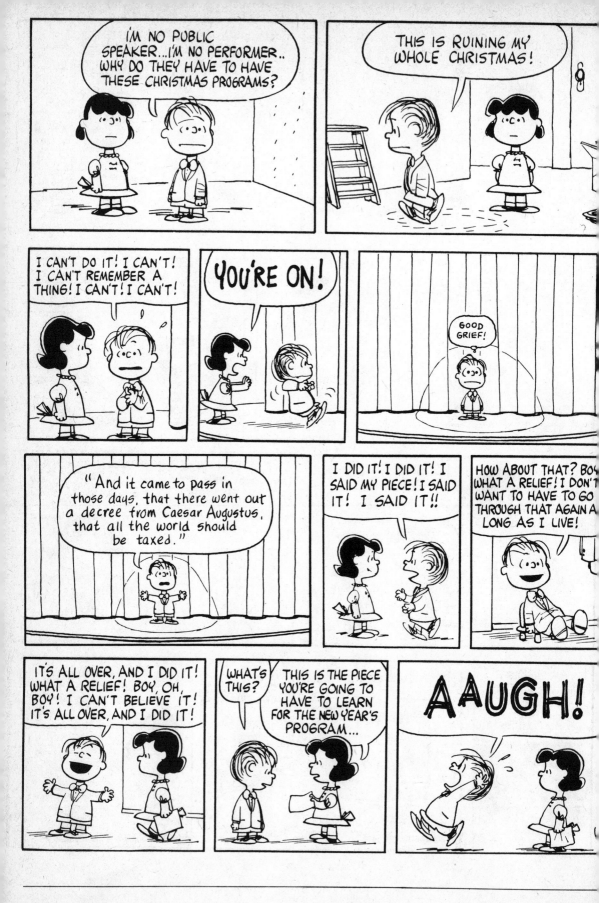

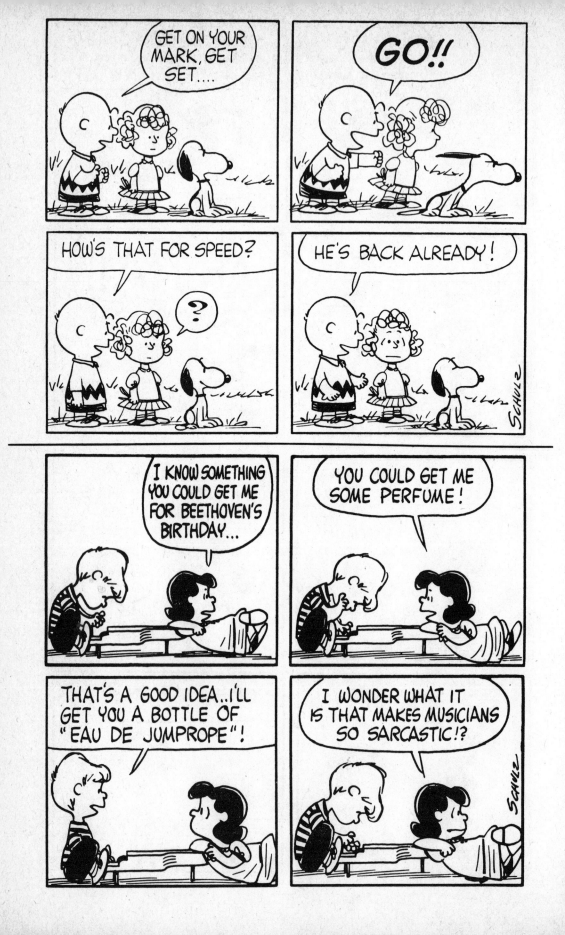

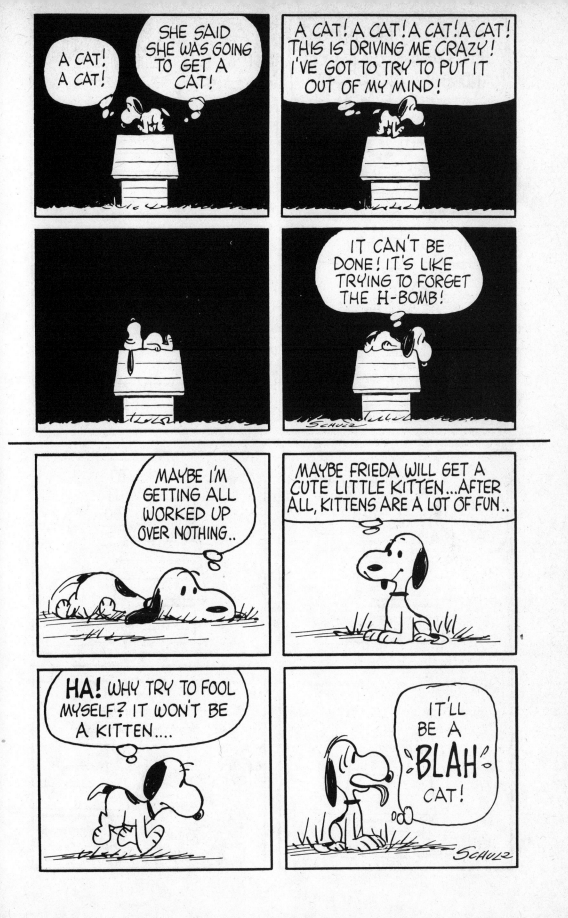

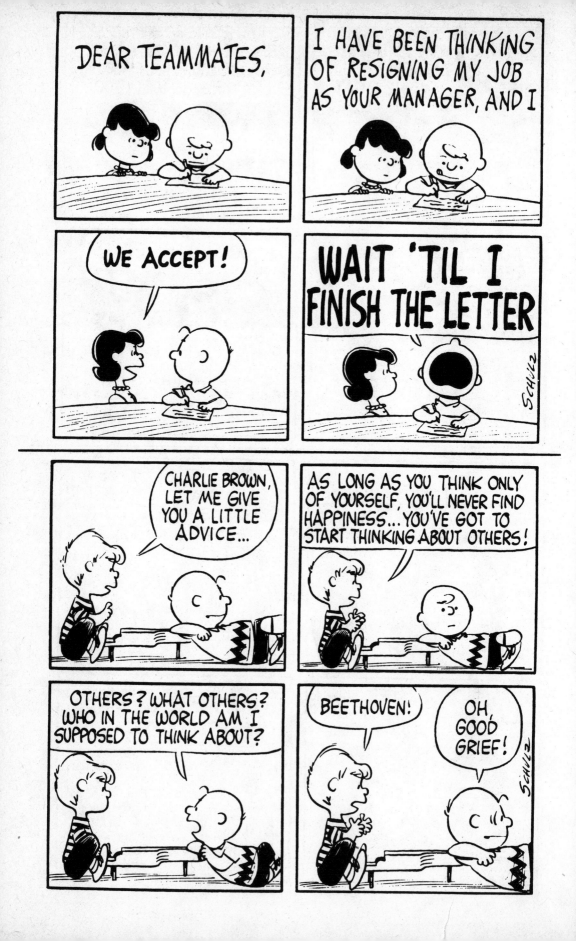

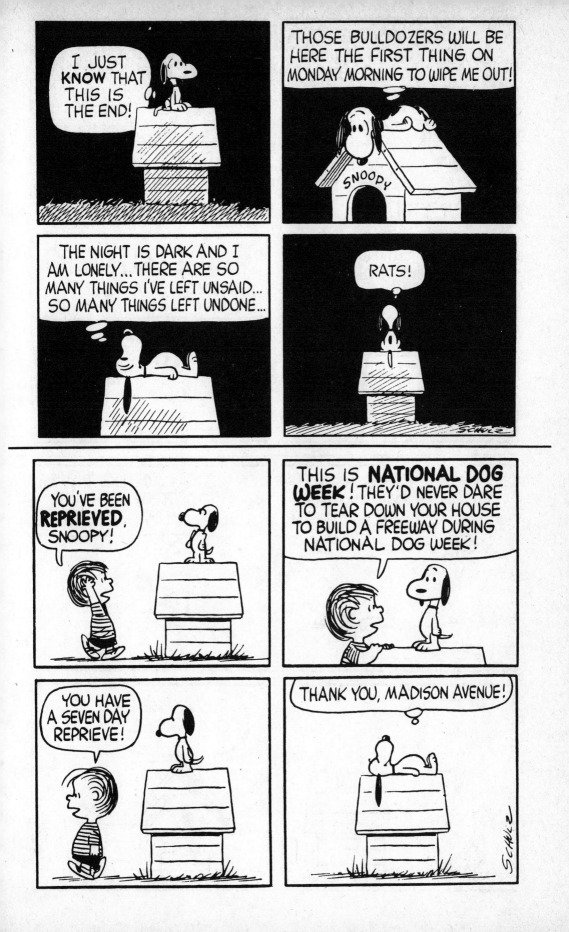

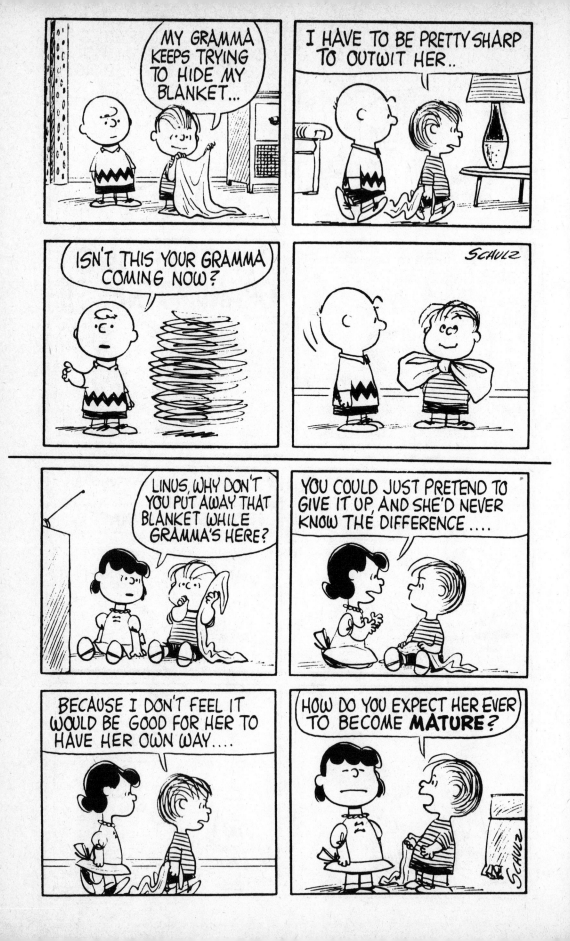